HEALING WORDS

AIMÉE FADOR

Illustrated by Michele Snell

ISBN 978-1-68526-994-4 (Paperback)
ISBN 978-1-68526-996-8 (Hardcover)
ISBN 978-1-68526-995-1 (Digital)

Covenant Books
11661 Hwy 707
Murrells Inlet, SC 29576
www.covenantbooks.com

To my husband, Steve, you are my world, my light, my best friend…the one whom my soul loves! I love us and the life we have built! You will forever be my always!

To our children, Liam and Gianna, I thank God every day for choosing me to be your mom. I have loved you unconditionally since the moment I knew you were with me. Dad and I could not be prouder of you both!

To my mom, Alice, my brothers, Jonathan and Timothy, and all my family, thank you for your support, your unconditional love, your prayers, and all of the beauty that is our family! My heart bursts with love for each of you!

To my friends, you are my chosen family, and I thank you for the countless memories, the loyalty, the endless laughter, and the love we all share!

To every child/teenager I have had the immense pleasure and honor of working with as a coach and teacher, you have taught me incredible lessons through the years, and I am forever grateful to know each and every one of you! Anyone who has the ability to work with children is blessed beyond measure. I often feel as though adults do not give our youth the credit they deserve. The mind of a child/teenager is sharp, attentive, perceptive, and wiser than we all realize, especially while they navigate the formidable chapters of their lives! The characters in this story emulate the beauty I have seen on so many occasions while working with this population, and I am a better person because of it!

A special thanks to my Poppy (my grandfather). You were the man who taught me what a gentleman is, how a lady should be treated, the importance of doing something to the best of your ability (at all times), and how being on time is actually late. You taught me what glorious adventures await you inside the pages of a book. You spent countless hours discussing with me our gorgeous Sicilian roots, athletics, and what it means to be an American; including but not limited to the importance of authentic, heartfelt patriotism, knowing the truth of our country's history, the significance of being educated, the American dream, and the policies of being a staunch Constitutionalist! You were incredibly intelligent, admired by all who knew you, and so very humble and kind…always. You instilled in me the core values I carry in my heart to this day, and I love you so!

To God be the glory!

"Can we all meet up by the tree?" Jess texted her friends in their group chat.
One by one, the friends in the group reply, "Yes."

Jess

Ben

Jake

Lisa

Ally

Dawn

Dominic

Kevin

Can we all meet up by the tree?

Yes

Yes

Yes

Yes

Yes

Yes

1

"Awesome," Jess texts back. "I'm throwing my shoes on and will head over there right now."

2

"Thanks for coming to hang out for a while, guys. I was in need of some friend time but didn't feel like watching a movie or going anywhere," Jess said. "I have been feeling so down lately, and I wanted to lean on you guys. Talk things out."

"I am so done with how angry everyone is! There are so many rules that don't even make sense, and everyone is so quick to say things, no matter how harsh, abrasive, or hurtful. I am tired of people bullying other people for thinking or feeling differently. I am tired of seeing friendships and relationships end horribly because one person said something that 'triggered' the other person. It is taking a toll on my family, friends, and really…everything and everyone," Jess said. Her voice shook with passion, and a tear rolled down her cheek.

4

There was silence for a moment or two, and then one of her friends spoke up.

"Jess, I couldn't agree more!" replied Ben. "I have family members who won't even speak to each other any longer. It is heartbreaking! My family has always been so close, and now I can't even remember the last time we all had dinner together, celebrated a birthday, or even a holiday with everyone present."

"Ben, I am so sorry your family is going through that," Jess replied with sincerity. "How your family is handling this polarizing time is not an isolated incident. I believe there are millions of families struggling right now, and it is so tragic!"

Jake sat up a little straighter and chimed in, "I just talked to my grandfather about all this the other day. The news is always on in our home, and it usually causes everyone who is there to start yelling and getting upset about politicians, or the salon down the street who will only let you in if you have a mask on, or the rising cost of gas, or how everything is more expensive if you can even find what you need at the store… you name it, it is a fair game for everyone to get all riled up about. I usually join in, but the other day I noticed my grandfather, who is normally one of the first to yell on the top of his lungs about 'all that is wrong with this world,' was being very quiet. I asked him if he wanted to go sit with me on the porch for a while."

7

Jake took a deep breath and continued, "My grandfather sat down on the rocking chair next to me, with his coffee mug in hand, and said this to me, 'You know what, Jake? The world is in complete disarray. I feel it in my heart and in my bones, and I am tired from it all.'"

Jake replied, "I know exactly what you mean, Pop. How did it get so bad? How did we let things get to this point?"

Jake's grandfather sat and pondered this question for a while as he rocked slightly. He took a comforting sip of his warm coffee and said, "The way things are today was bound to happen. Life isn't simple anymore. People complicate everything and the things that should be focused on have become lost, cast to the side, ignored… forgotten. Being disciplined, proud, happy, patriotic, faith-filled, hardworking, selfless—these aren't qualities that we should fondly remember as the way people once were, but instead, those characteristics are what everyone should have. A smile as you walk past someone should be automatic just like a friendly wave as you drive by. Holding the door for the person or people behind you. A firm handshake. Looking people in the eyes when talking or being spoken to. Saying 'sir' and 'ma'am.' Helping someone without ever expecting anything in return. You are a good young man, Jake, and you know all of this already but this old man, well, I am just tired seeing so many who do not."

Jake was about to speak but noticed a far-off look in his Pop's eyes. He actually hoped his grandfather would continue to speak because of everyone in Jake's life, his Pop was his most favorite. His grandfather didn't disappoint.

"I remember the very day I enlisted. I didn't even think twice about it. My father served and so did my uncles. My oldest brother, who was my best friend, served, and I just always remember being filled with so much pride whenever I saw the flag. It made me feel close to my brother even when he was somewhere thousands of miles away. The flag made me think of how proud I felt inside when my dad and his war buddies would get together, as if no time had passed, and fill the air with stories and laughter and sometimes silence and heaviness that felt as if you could reach out and touch it. Their time together caused the kind of tears to form that make the back of your throat ache. To this day, I still get a lump in my throat when I see a breeze blow old glory beautifully back and forth or I hear the words of our nation's anthem. I was willing to do whatever it took to keep our country safe, even if that meant dying for her and all who live here. If I had my life to live all over again, I would make the same decision without hesitation. But you want to know why I was so confident in my choice to enlist?" he asked.

"Yes, sir. I do want to know," Jake answered.

"I was so confident because I have always known God ever since I was a little boy, and I knew this nation was and is the greatest country because of Him. God has a plan for us all, and He is the one in control. When we trust in Him, no matter what heartache, challenges, tragedy, or fears we experience along the way, He is always with us. No matter where life takes us, He is always with us. I knew I would never be alone when on the battlefield somewhere so very far from the comforts and familiarity of home. Knowing that has been the only thing to bring me consistent comfort every day of my life, even on the darkest days, and I have had my fair share. You remember that, Jake! You remember that no matter how bad the day or the coming days may seem, you are never alone. Trust in Him, Jake! Be a man of faith and walk your path through life with love, faith, and a strong relationship with God. If you do that, kindness, respect, and wholesomeness will be your strongest characteristics. That is what the world needs more of. That is what people have forgotten and nothing is ever going to get better unless people turn back to God."

Jake, with tears in his eyes, looked at his grandfather and said, "You have my word, Pop. I will be a man of God and will do my part to help others walk a life of faith, also."

Jess speaks up. "This is exactly why I texted all of you. I needed to hear those words from you, Jake. Next time you see your grandfather, please give him a hug for me!"

13

Dawn, who was leaning against the tree, suggested they all bow their heads and pray together.

"I have known you guys since I was two," Dominic said, "but you know I don't even go to church. I appreciate what your grandfather said to you, Jake, and I do believe in God, but I don't even know Him. I certainly don't feel comfortable saying a prayer, even if it is with my best friends. I don't even know what to say."

It was Ally who spoke up then and said, "Dom, praying to God is just like having a conversation with any of us. You don't need to say a formal prayer you memorized, you just speak what is in your heart and He will always listen. The best part is, if you speak from your heart and quiet your mind, sometimes you can even hear Him answer you back. It may take a while for your prayers to be answered but that is because God's timing is not always our timing. He knows every moment of our lives already, so it is up to us to trust Him fully. He loves you and all of us so very much. We must work on trusting His plan and building a beautiful relationship with Him which begins with having conversations with Him every chance we can!"

Dominic remained quiet. He looked down at his hands as he fiddled with a leaf he picked up from the ground. Lisa quietly snuggled up beside him and laid her head on his shoulder. All the friends sat in silence for a few moments. They could hear the foghorn hum its familiar tune in the distance. They could hear the chirping of the birds and the rustle of leaves as a squirrel leapt from one branch to the next overhead. They could feel the crisp autumn breeze tickle their skin and the warmth of the sun's rays as it occasionally broke through the clouds above.

"God, if You are listening…well, I guess I know You are listening," Dawn said quietly. "Help us, help our families and all our friends hear from You and feel Your presence. The world kind of stinks right now. There is so much hate. So many things tempt us to fill our thoughts with evil. Too many people are listening to the wrong messages, listening to the wrong sources. Too many people, Lord, myself included at times, walk with fear and anger. Help us, please, Lord."

Ben took Dawn's hand and said, "I usually don't talk to You, God, unless I am sitting at service on Sunday, and I am sorry for that. I am sorry for allowing anger to get the best of me so much lately and for judging other people. It is hard to not think things about others when you hear them talking behind your back. I try to keep my head down, do the right thing, but sometimes I just want to scream. It is hard, Lord,

to not question even Your plan because the world is struggling right now and some days are just really, really, hard."

Lisa, still leaning on Dom's shoulder, spoke next. "Lord, I didn't give my life to You until a few short years ago. When I lost my father to cancer… I watched him wither into a person I couldn't even recognize. To see his face somber and no longer with his infectious smile or gentleness, I felt my heart shatter. I didn't think I would ever be able to laugh, love or really feel anything but that numbness, that anger, and that completely engulfing sensation of deep grief and sadness.

"My grandmother brought me to church with her, and although all those who were around me were participating, singing, worshiping You… I could only sit and listen. I watched my grandmother, who was losing her only son to an unforgiving disease, smile, cry, and love You with all her being throughout the service. You gave me so much to think about, Lord. I cried myself to sleep that night and spent my next day oh so quiet. I started listening to those around me, paying attention to the words that came from their mouths, their body language and actions, and how I felt around certain people. I started wondering if the things I was saying, thinking, and doing were wrong, right, or somewhere in between. I couldn't wait to go to church again that following Sunday and that yearning became stronger and stronger as the weeks went by. Before I knew it, I was on my feet worshiping You and praising You, praying to You daily, and feeling the heaviness of a grief so deep become less a burden with each passing day. I trust in You, Lord, and I love You. You gave me this group of friends whom I can be myself around. You have given me so much, and even now, when I feel as though the world is holding onto the heaviness I once carried, I know You will rescue all who come to You. Your love knows no bounds. Your Kingdom welcomes all." When Lisa stopped praying, she realized that at some point, Dom had put her hand in his.

Kevin, who up until this point hadn't said a word, cleared his throat and took a deep breath. "Uh…hey, God. I don't normally just start talking to You, but I'm beginning to think that is exactly what I need to do. I'm pretty quiet, my friends here will tell You that but then again, You know everything about me so, uh, I guess… um…man, I'm making a mess of this," Kevin said, shaking his head.

Jess said gently, "You are doing great, Kev." Just say whatever comes to your mind or whatever is in your heart."

Clearing his throat nervously, Kevin started to speak once more, "Okay, let me try this again. I don't feel the need to say too much because I think everyone around me says just about everything they feel compelled to…sometimes a little too much in my opinion, and I don't feel the need to put in my two cents. Lately, as I have sat back listening, I have heard more and more, I don't like. I have more questions than answers, and I think too many people aren't willing to listen like they should. Instead, everyone is just too quick to say what they want to say without even thinking about their words first. I have seen firsthand what harsh words can do to other people, including myself, and I ask You, Lord, help people to take a breath. Help them to take a moment to think before they speak. Words have power. Words have consequences. It is not okay to lie, slander, or to make others feel less of themselves. I love our Constitution, Lord, but please help people realize that even with our great First Amendment, everyone needs to have some self-control. Everyone needs to have a filter. Everyone just needs to think before they speak." Kevin was speaking less nervously now, and his voice rang out with the truth. His friends all looked upon their usually quiet friend's face with awe as Kevin continued.

"My grandmother used to say, 'people are like a bouquet of wildflowers. All perfectly and beautifully made and how great that is because if we all looked the same, how boring the world would be.' Well I believe that holds true for how people think differently, too. We don't all need to think the same, look the same, act the same, believe the same things, and in no way should anyone be forced to do anything that goes against all they believe. But we all need to remember that we are Your children, You make no mistakes, and we need to love and respect each other. Please, God… help."

"Wow!" Jess said. "Hard to follow that one, Kev. That was awesome!" All the friends smiled at their tender-hearted and quiet friend and uttered words of agreement.

"Well," Jess started again, "when I asked my friends to come to our tree…the place we started hanging out so many years ago. The place where some of our first play dates were while our parents hung out on blankets spread out on the ground and we were still in diapers…never did I think we would all end up here praying together. We have never done this before, and I didn't even know that this is what I needed, but I know it is exactly as my heart desired. I think I really feel Your presence here with us right now because I have a feeling of peace, and I haven't felt this way in a really long time.

"I feel like the world has become flipped upside down, and I don't know how much longer it can stay this way before things really get bad. I haven't been able to see family members who live out of state for so long because they live in a constant state of fear or they are unwilling to spend time with my parents, siblings, and me because we think differently about all that is going on in this country and abroad. I am tired of never being able to see people's full faces because they are always covered with a mask. The eyes that peer back at me are cold, fatigued, distant, or, more often than not, averted as to not even make contact. I am tired of never being able to turn on the tv, the radio, or overhear a conversation in line at the coffee shop without feeling as though a one-sided opinion, no matter what side of the aisle it lies, is getting jammed down my throat. But in Your presence right now, with friends who are like family, I am reminded of Your plan. I am reminded to trust in You always and maybe the reason the world is upside down is because so many have forgotten that, too! I promise to spend more time with You, Lord, and in turn, I want anyone around me to feel Your presence through me. Use me Lord to help others be reminded of Your unconditional love and to trust in You fully! Help me to bring others to You, Lord, so we can turn the world right side up!"

Dom squeezed Lisa's hand a little tighter, and Lisa squeezed back.

"I want to start by saying thank You, Jesus. Thank You for giving us our lives here in the greatest country in the world. Thank You for bringing us all together. Thank You for this powerful moment right here and right now," Jake spoke with emotion in his voice. "Please do not let the noise of the world keep us from hearing Your voice. I want You to show me how to take the person I am, the person You want me to be, and help me to do all I can in my life for a purpose greater than myself. I think there is evil at play right now and You, and You alone, are the answer. Please help our nation turn to You. Let a revival come upon this world and let all of us who give our lives to You and invite the Holy Spirit to reside in us, do everything while giving You full praise." Tears fell down Jake's face as he kept his eyes closed and hands stretched up to the sky.

All the friends raised their hands to the sky, Dominic included. They sat like that, sunbeams dancing upon their faces, for several minutes. Before Dominic opened his eyes, he let tears silently fall and with a quivering voice he said out loud, "Amen."

At that moment, Jess knew it was God who compelled her to pick up the phone and text her friends that afternoon and she was so very thankful she did. They all needed this time. They all needed these prayers and healing words.

The friends all stood, hugged each other, gathered their things, and walked silently to their cars. Just as Dom was about to get into his truck, he called out to his friends, "Same time tomorrow, guys?" Each friend agreed without hesitation. Dom smiled and climbed into his truck and shut the door. Before putting the key into the ignition, he said aloud for only God to hear, "I look forward to talking tomorrow, God." He smiled, fired up his truck, and gave his friends a loving little wave as he headed home.

Father God,

I boldly pray for the United States of America. I pray for all American citizens to quiet the noise of the world…quiet the negativity, and all doubt. I pray that people from coast to coast draw nearer to You so Your love, grace, and peace settle in their hearts replacing the fear, guilt, and anger they carry with them like a chain that makes each step a burden.

Under Your grace and unconditional love, let people become born again bringing them into a new life…a life with You as their priority. You as their Father. You as their *everything*!

Help us all to remember that You and You alone are in control and that we all have a duty to live the life You have planned for us with patience, kindness, and faith. Help us to remember You knew us before we were born...

> *Before I formed you in the womb I knew you, and before you were born I consecrated you; I appointed you a prophet to the nations. (Jeremiah 1:5 ESV)*

> *Your eyes saw my unformed substance; in your book were written, every one of them, the days that were formed for me, when as yet there was none of them. (Psalm 139:16 ESV)*

And that You make no mistakes. We all matter. We all have purpose.

> *I praise you because I am fearfully and wonderfully made; your works are wonderful; I know that full well. (Psalm 139:14 NIV)*

Lord, help us to find compassion in our hearts and forgiveness. You have blessed us with the beautiful ability to think freely but with that comes great responsibility and that includes not only Your guidance for our actions but also our thoughts and words.

I ask for wisdom, Lord. I yearn to learn more from You so that I may help others come to You and so that others may see You in me. Help me to be a leader of love and light. Help me to welcome the Holy Spirit inside me and for others to do the same!

I want to cover all our military, law enforcement, and first responders in prayer, Lord. Watch over them with grace and protection. Help any misguided information that has been placed upon their ears become silenced and may their hearts be strengthened, as well as their understanding through their righteous place as protectors.

> *Blessed are the peacemakers, for they will be called children of God. (Matthew 5:9 NIV)*

I pray that families strengthen in unity and in that togetherness make You the head of their family always. Guide families, including my own, to have open hearts and courage to stand up for what is right and to stay the course when they are challenged.

But from everlasting to everlasting the Lord's love is with those who fear him and his righteousness with their children's children—with those who keep his covenant and remember to obey his precepts. (Psalm 103:17–18 NIV)

The wicked die and disappear, but the family of the godly stands firm. (Proverbs 12:7 NLT)

I pray that friends, true friends, end any self-doubt or fear of being their true selves amongst each other. Let hearts be open to receive us as we are, to love and accept us as You have made us, and to not cast judgment, as that is Your job and Your job alone!

The godly give good advice to their friends, the wicked lead them astray. (Proverbs 12:26 NLT)

Two people are better off than one, for they can help each other succeed. If one person falls, the other can reach out and help. But someone who falls alone is in real trouble. Likewise, two people lying close together can keep each other warm. But how can one be warm alone? A person standing alone can be attacked and defeated, but two can stand back-to-back and conquer. Three are even better, for a triple-braided cord is not easily broken. (Ecclesiastes 4:9–12 NLT)

Lord, I ask for you to bless me and others with courage and the wisdom to discern between good and evil. Guide our thoughts, words, and actions so they are pleasing to You. Help us to help others without ever needing recognition or expecting anything in return. Help humility to capture the lives of those who walk in Your grace. Help us to stay strong and when challenges and troubling times come upon us, and they will, Lord, help us to keep our eyes on You and to not lose faith but instead rejoice and give You praise, especially on the darkest of days. For You, Lord, will always bring us to the light!

I pray in earnest for this nation that we may stand united. Eliminate the division that is occurring and the acts of despair, sacrilege, and evil from this great country! Help us as one nation under You so that we may rise above all evil and reaffirm our foundation which is You, O Lord! Guide leaders to not fail their constituents, guide them to lead with morality and integrity. Be just, Lord, as You always are!

And I thank You, Lord. I thank You for forgiving us of all past transgressions when we lay our true repentance at Your feet. I thank You for loving us with a love that is immeasurable. I thank You for each lesson You have taught along the way… every obstacle, every challenge, every sorrow, and heartache. In all of these lessons, I was never alone, and the sun always shone, once again. Though I may be weary, I take comfort in knowing You are seated at the right hand of the Father, and You are with me always! We are not meant to walk through life alone, we are meant to walk with You and in doing so, the short time on earth is a blessing…a precursor to a blessed life of eternity. I love You and worship You with all my soul!

In Jesus's name, I pray! Amen.

ABOUT THE ILLUSTRATOR

Michele Snell, born and raised in New York, has resided in Savannah, Georgia since 1996. She is an accomplished muralist and has many murals in commercial, public, and residential establishments. She is also known for the local sceneries and wildlife she captures in oils on canvas, as well as her popularity in creating lifelike pet portraits.

In addition to her work shown here in this book, more of Michele's work can be found on her Facebook page, Michele Snell Gallery, and on her website, www.michelesnellart.com.

ABOUT THE AUTHOR

An avid reader with an old soul, Aimée Fador is a new author who dreams of creating treasures for years to come. Aimee, her husband Steve, and their children, Liam and Gianna, all born and raised New Englanders spent a brief period of time living on the Georgia coast. It was during this time spent in the Low Country this book came to fruition, before heading back to their home in New England. Authenticity and morality are prominent pillars in Aimée's professional and personal life! She is not shy in sharing her emotions, her compassion, her loyalty, and her walk in faith. Aimée weaves her beliefs and her passions throughout the journey she takes her readers on. It is a journey that is both tangible and relatable for all ages, especially in a time where love, faith, and healing words are needed by all.

CPSIA information can be obtained
at www.ICGtesting.com
Printed in the USA
BVHW012029120223
658300BV00017B/525